Mission Furniture - Part II

1910

HENRY HAVEN WINDSOR

TABLE OF CONTENTS

NOTE

This book is one of the series of handbooks on industrial subjects being published by the Popular Mechanics Co. Like the magazine, these books are "written so you can understand it," and are intended to furnish information on mechanical subjects at a price within the reach of all.

The texts and illustrations have been prepared expressly for this Handbook Series, by experts; are up-to-date, and have been revised by the editor of Popular Mechanics.

The dimensions given in the stock list contained in the description of each piece of furniture illustrated in this book call for material mill-planed, sanded and cut to length. If the workman

desires to have a complete home-made article, allowance must be made in the dimensions for planing and squaring the pieces. S-4-S and S-2-S are abbreviations for surface four sides and surface two sides.

PART I. AN OAK BUFFET

AN OAK BUFFET

The accompanying sketch and detail drawing show a design of a buffet wherein refinement of outline and harmony of details are conspicuously regarded. Quarter-sawed oak is the most suitable wood for this handsome piece of mission furniture. The material should be ordered from the mill ready cut to length, squared and sanded. Following is a list of the stock needed:

2 back posts, 2 by 2 by 47-3/4 in.
2 front posts, 2 by 2 by 45-1/2 in.
4 rails, 1-1/2 by 1-1/2 by 50-1/2 in.
2 end rails, 1-1/2 by 1-1/2 by 18-1/2 in.
4 end rails, 3/4 by 4 by 18-1/2 in.
4 pieces for end panel, 3/4 by 3-1/2 by 21 in.
2 panels, 3/8 by 12 by 21 in.
1 top board, 3/4 by 17-1/2 by 47-1/4 in.
1 back board, 3/4 by 11-1/2 by 47-1/4 in.
1 shelf board, 3/4 by 2 by 46 in.
2 brackets, 1 by 2 by 7-3/4 in.
4 pieces for doors, 3/4 by 4 by 11 in.
2 panels, 3/8 by 11 by 17-1/2 in.
1 piece for drawer, 3/4 by 8 by 22-1/2 in.
1 piece for drawer, 3/4 by 7-1/2 by 22-1/2 in.
1 piece for drawer, 3/4 by 7 by 22-1/2 in.
2 pieces, 1/2 by 8 by 19-1/4 in.; soft wood.
2 pieces, 1/2 by 7-1/2 by 19-1/4 in.; soft wood.
2 pieces, 1/2 by 7 by 19-1/4 in.; soft wood.
1 piece, 1/2 by 8 by 19-1/4 in.; soft wood.

1 piece, 1/2 by 7-1/2 by 19-1/4 in.; soft wood.
1 piece, 1/2 by 7 by 19-1/4 in.; soft wood.
1 bottom board, 3/4 by 17-1/2 by 47-1/4 in.; soft wood.
2 partitions (several pieces), 3/4 by 20 by 24-3/4 in.
2 front pieces, 3/4 by 2 by 23 in.
2 back pieces. 3/4 by 2 by 23 in.; soft wood.
2 side pieces, 3/4 by 2 by 21-1/2 in.; soft wood.
1 back (several pieces), 3/8 by 25 by 46 in.
1 mirror frame (to suit mirror).

Start to work on the four posts by squaring them up to the proper length in pairs and beveling the tops as shown. Clamp all four pieces on a flat surface with the bottom ends even, then lay out the mortises for the rails and panels on all four pieces at once with a try-square. This insures getting the mortises all the same height. The back posts also have a mortise cut in them at the top for the back board as shown. Lay out the tenons on the ends of the front and back rails in the same manner. Cut them to fit the mortises in the posts, also rabbet the back rails for the backing. Cut tenons on the end rails and rabbet them and the side pieces for the panels.

Lay out the top and bottom boards to the proper size and notch the corners to fit about the posts. These boards are fastened to the 1-1/2-in. square rails with dowels and glue. They can now be glued together and set away to dry. The top board is of oak, and be sure to get the best side up, while the bottom one can be made of soft wood if desired.

The partitions are made of several boards glued together. Be careful to get an oak board on the outer edge. The drawer slides are set into the partitions as shown and are fastened in place with screws from the inside.

The top back board has a tenon on each end that fits into the mortises in the back posts and is rounded at the top as shown. The shelf is also rounded at the ends and is fastened to the back with screws.

A plate glass mirror should be provided for the back. This is fitted to the back board as shown, then the brackets put up at the ends of the mirror frame.

The main parts are now ready to be assembled and glued together. Before applying any glue, see that all the joints fit together perfectly. The end rails and the panels are glued together first and allowed to dry. Be very careful to get the parts clamped together perfectly square and straight, else you will have trouble later on. When these ends are dry slip them on the tenons on the front and back rails which are already fastened to the top and bottom boards.

The back board and the partitions must be in place when this is done. Pin and glue the joints and clamp the whole together square and leave to dry.

The doors are now made by mortising the top and bottom pieces to take the 3/8-in. panel which is glued in place. The drawers are made as shown in the sketch. The front board should be oak, but the remainder can be made of soft wood. The joints are nailed and glued. Suitable hinges for the doors and handles for the drawers should be provided. Antique copper trimmings look very well with this style of furniture and can be secured at most any hardware store.

The back is made of soft wood and is put on in the usual manner. Scrape all surplus glue from about the joints, as stain will not take where there is any glue. Finish smooth with fine sandpaper, then apply the stain you like best. This can be any one of the many mission stains supplied by the trade for this purpose.

OAK STAIN

An easy and at the same time a good way to stain oak in imitation of the fumed effect, is to boil catechu in the proportion of 1/4 lb. to 6 lb. of water, after which cool and strain. Apply this to the wood, and when dry treat with a solution of bichromate of potash in the same proportion as with the catechu. Bichromate of potash alone in water will give a good stain. A solution of 2 oz. of pearl ash and 2 oz. of potash mixed in a quart of water makes a good stain. Potash solution darkens the wood, and when applied very strong will produce an almost ebon hue, due to what we might describe as the burning of the wood fiber.

A PLAIN OAK HALL CLOCK

The hall clock shown in the illustration should be made of plain oak. The following pieces will be needed to make it:
2 back posts, 1-1/2 by 1-1/2 by 81 in., S-4-S.
2 front posts, 1-1/2 by 1-1/2 by 21 in., S-4-S.
2 front posts, 1-1/2 by 1-1/2 by 44 in., S-4-S.
10 front and back horizontals, 1-1/2 by 1-1/2 by 15 in., S-4-S.
10 side horizontals, 1-1/2 by 1-1/2 by 11 in., S-4-S.
1 face, 3/8 by 14 by 14 in., S-4-S.

Front Doors

4 rails, 3/4 by 1-1/2 by 18 in., S-4-S.
4 stiles, 3/4 by 1-1/2 by 12 in., S-4-S.
4 horizontal mullions, 3/16 by 3/4 by 11 in., S-4-S.
4 horizontal mullions, 3/16 by 5/8 by 11 in., S-4-S.
4 vertical mullions, 3/16 by 3/4 by 15 in., S-4-S.
2 vertical mullions, 3/16 by 5/8 by 15 in., S-4-S.

Back

1 piece, 3/8 by 14 by 21 in., S-4-S.
2 pieces, 3/8 by 14 by 18 in., S-4-S.
4 horizontal mullions, 3/16 by 5/8 by 14 in., S-4-S.
4 vertical mullions, 3/16 by 5/8 by 20 in., S-4-S.

Top Side Panels

2 pieces, 3/8 by 9-1/2 by 14 in., S-4-S.
8 horizontal mullions, 3/16 by 5/8 by 9-1/2 in., S-4-S.
6 vertical mullions, 3/16 by 5/8 by 14 in., S-4-S.
2 middle side panels, 3/4 by 9-1/2 by 20 in., S-2-S.

Lower Side Panels

8 vertical mullions, 3/16 by 3/4 by 18 in., S-4-S.
8 vertical mullions, 3/16 by 5/8 by 18 in., S-4-S.
8 horizontal mullions, 3/16 by 3/4 by 9-1/2 in., S-4-S.
8 horizontal mullions, 3/16 by 5/8 by 9-1/2 in., S-4-S.

If the worker will take the trouble to combine the different lengths of pieces having like thicknesses and widths into pieces of standard lengths, he will be able to save himself some expense at the mill with no more work for himself.

Begin work by shaping the ends of the posts as indicated in the drawing. Lay out and cut the mortises for the tenons of the horizontals or rails. These mortises need not be deep if the joints are to be reinforced later with lag screws as is the clock shown. They may be what are known as stub tenons and mortises. The tenons are not more than 1/2 in. long, just enough to keep the rail from turning about.

Next lay out and cut the tenons on the rails. Bore the holes for the lag screws, being careful to bore on adjacent surfaces so that the holes will miss each other. Use a 3/8 by 3-in. lag screw, boring the hole in the tenon with a 1/4-in. bit the full depth the screw is to enter.

The side panels should be fitted into grooves in the rails, and before the frame is put together these panels should be squared up and the grooves cut in the rails and posts at the proper places.

The mullions of the lower side panels, it will be noted, are specified 5/8 and 3/4 in. wide. The 5/8-in. pieces are for the central parts of the frame and the others for the outside. The frame is to be made 1/8 in. larger all around than the distance between the posts and between the rails so that it may be set in grooves cut in the posts and the rails to a similar depth, 1/8 in. This is true, also, of the mullions of the front doors. Square up the shelves so that they may be set into grooves in the adjacent rails. The middle shelf is to have an overhang and will rest upon the rails.

The mullions of the top side panels are all of the same width, and it is not intended or necessary to set their frame into grooves in the posts. The wood panel back of them gives ample strength.

It is a good plan not to groove the panel upon which the figures are placed, and which becomes the face of the clock. It is better to fit this piece in and fasten metal or wood buttons on the back side so that it can be readily taken off to get at the clock movement from the front.

Make the doors, tenoning the rails into the stiles and grooving both to receive the mullioned framework of 3/16-in. stuff.

Put the whole frame together, using good hot glue for the joints. When the glue has dried sufficiently to allow the clamps to be taken off, fit the doors and hinge them. Butterfly surface hinges look well and are the easiest to apply.

Thoroughly scrape all the surplus glue off and sandpaper the parts preparatory to applying the finish.

To finish, apply one coat of mission oak water stain. When dry, sandpaper lightly, using No. 00 paper. Apply a second coat, diluted with an equal amount of water. Sand this lightly and put on a very thin coat of shellac to keep the filler color, which follows, from discoloring the high lights. When the shellac has had time to harden, sand lightly and put on a coat of paste filler. Use light filler, colored with umber and Venetian red in the proportion of 12 oz, of umber, and 4 oz. of red to 20 lb. of filler. The directions for applying the filler will be found on the can labels. On the hardened filler apply a thin coat of shellac. Sand the shellac lightly and put on several coats of some good floor wax, polishing well according to the directions on the can. This is what is known as a mission oak finish and is quite popular for this type of furniture design.

The metal figures for the dial come with the clock movement. Some of the movements come already set in boxes of wood so that all one needs to do is to shape the projecting ends of the wood containing boxes and fasten them to the frame with screws from the back. A clock with dial figures, eight-day movement, striking the hours and half hours, with cathedral gong can be bought for $4, possibly less.

A ROCKING CHAIR

In furniture construction such as this, nothing is gained by trying to plane up the stock out of the rough. This is mere drudgery and can be more cheaply and easily done at the planing mill by machinery. There will be plenty to do to cut and fit all the different parts. Order the pieces mill-planed and sandpapered to the sizes specified below.

Plain sawed red oak takes a mission finish nicely and is appropriate. Some people like quartered white oak better, however. The cost is about the same.

The stock for the chair is as follows: Widths and thicknesses are specified exact except for the rear posts and the rockers; but to the lengths enough surplus stock has been added to allow for squaring the ends.

2 front posts, 1-5/8 by 2-1/4 by 22-1/2 in., S-4-S.

2 back posts, 1-5/8 by 11 by 40 in., S-2-S.

1 front horizontal, 3/4 by 3-1/2 by 22 in., S-4-S.

1 back horizontal, 3/4 by 3-1/2 by 20 in., S-4-S.

2 back horizontals, 3/4 by 3-1/2 by 20 in., S-4-S.

2 side horizontals, 3/4 by 3-1/2 by 20 in., S-4-S.

2 back slats, 5/16 by 3-1/2 by 20 in., S-4-S.

2 arms, 1 by 4-1/2 by 25 in., S-2-S.

1 rocker, 2-1/4 by 6 by 33 in., S-2-S.

5 bottom slats, 3/4 by 2-1/2 by 19-1/2 in., S-4-S.

Begin work on the posts first. The front posts should have one end of each squared, after which they can be cut to the exact length. The rear posts, according to the stock bill, are specified for the exact thickness. By exercising forethought, both may be got from the piece ordered. The tops and bottoms of the posts should have their edges slightly chamfered to prevent their slivering.

The shape of the arm is a little out of the ordinary, but the drawing indicates quite clearly how it is cut. The arm is fastened to the posts by means of dowels and glue after the other parts of the chair have been put together.

Now prepare the curved parts of the back. These parts are worked to size, after which they are thoroughly steamed and bent in the forms described on another page. These forms should have a surface curve whose radius is 22 in. While the parts are drying out, go ahead with the cutting of the mortises and tenons of post and rail.

Inasmuch as the width of the front of the chair exceeds that of the back by 2 in., allowance must be made for slant either in the tenons of the side rails or in the mortises. This will necessitate the use of the bevel in laying off the shoulders of the tenons.

The slats for the bottom are made long enough so that their ends may be "let into" the front and back rails, a 3/4-in. groove being plowed to receive them.

Assemble the back, then the front; and when the glue on them has dried, put the side rails in place, then the arms. The chair should now be scraped and sandpapered preparatory to applying the finish.

The cushion shown in the picture is made of Spanish roan skin leather and is filled with elastic felt. Such cushions can be purchased at the upholsterer's or they can be made by the craftsman himself. Frequently the two parts of the cushion are laced together by means of leather thongs.

A CURVED BACK ARM CHAIR

The arm chair, the picture and drawing of which is given herewith is a companion piece to the rocker described on another page.

With the exception of the back-legs the stock bill which follows gives the thicknesses and widths exact. To the length, however, enough has been added to allow squaring up the ends.

Plain sawed white or red oak will be suitable for a design such as this.

Front posts, 2 pieces, 1-5/8 by 2-1/4 by 26 in., S-4-S.

Back posts, 1 piece, 1-5/8 by 8 by 45 in., S-2-S.

Front horizontals, 2 pieces, 3/4 by 3-1/2 by 21-1/2 in., S-4-S.

Rear horizontals, 4 pieces, 3/4 by 3-1/2 by 19-1/4 in., S-4-S.

Side horizontals, 4 pieces, 3/4 by 3-1/2 by 19-1/2 in., S-4-S.

Back slats, 2 pieces, 5/16 by 3-1/2 by 19-1/2 in., S-4-S.

Arms, 2 pieces, 1-1/8 by 4 by 24 in., S-4-S.

Seat slats, 5 pieces, 1/2 by 2-1/4 by 20 in., S-4-S.

Begin work by squaring up the ends of the front posts and shaping the rear ones Chamfer the ends of the tops and bottoms slightly so that they shall not splinter through usage. Next lay out the mortises and tenons.

The curved horizontals for the back should now be prepared and steamed as described on another page. The curved form to which the steamed piece is to be clamped to give shape to it should be curved slightly more than is wanted in the piece, as the piece when released will tend to straighten a little.

The arms of the chair may be shaped while these pieces are drying on the forms. The rails of the front and back may be tenoned, too. It should be noted that the front of the chair is wider than the back. This will necessitate care in mortising and tenoning the side rails so as to get good fits for the shoulders The bevel square will be needed in laying out the shoulders of the tenons.

Assemble the back, then the front. When the glue has hardened on these parts so that the clamps may be removed, put in the side rails or horizontals and again adjust the clamps. The arms are to be fastened to the posts with dowels and glue.

The seat, it will be seen from the drawing, is to be a loose leather cushion to rest upon slats. These seat slats may be fastened to cleats which have been previously fastened to the inside of the front and back seat rails or they may be "let in" to these rails by grooving their inner surfaces before the rails have been put in place. The latter method is more workmanlike, but more difficult.

A cushion such as is shown can be purchased ready made up, or it may be made by the amateur by lacing together two pieces of Spanish leather cut to size and punched along the edges so as to allow a lacing of leather thong. It may be filled with hair or elastic felt such as upholsterers use.

Probably the simplest finish that can be used is weathered oak. Put on a coat of weather oak oil stain, sandpaper lightly when dry and then put on a very thin coat of shellac. Sand this lightly and follow with two or more coats of floor wax put on in very thin coatings and polished well.

A PLATE RACK

The plate rack shown in the accompanying illustration is designed for use in a room furnished in mission style. The dimensions may be changed to suit the wall space. The parts are held together entirely by keys. The bar across the front is for keeping the plates from falling out, but this may be left out if the plates are allowed to lean against the wall.

The following list of material will be needed, and, if the builder does not care to do the rough work, the stock can be ordered planed, sanded and cut to the exact size of the dimensions given.

2 ends, 7/8 by 5 by 20 in.
1 top, 7/8 by 6 by 36 in.
1 shelf, 7/8 by 5 by 36 in.
1 bar, 7/8 in. square by 36 in.
4 keys. Scrap pieces will do.

Lay out and cut the mortises on the end pieces for the tenons of the shelf, also the tenons on the top ends and the diamond shaped openings. In laying these out, work from the back edge of the pieces. Cut the tenons on the ends of the shelf to fit the mortises in the end pieces, numbering each one so the parts can be put together with the tenons in the proper mortises. Mark out and cut the mortises in the top to receive the tenons on the end pieces.

In laying out the mortises for the keys allow a little extra on the side toward the shoulder so the ends and tops may be drawn up tightly when the keys are driven in the mortises. All the mortises and diamond shaped openings should be marked and cut with a chisel from both sides of the board.

If the bar is used, it may be attached with a flat side or edge out as shown.

Finish the pieces separately with any weathered or fumed oak stain. When thoroughly dry, apply a very thin coat of shellac. Finish with two coats of wax. The rack can be attached to the wall by two mirror plates fastened on the back edges of the end pieces.

PART II. TOOL FOR MARKING DOWEL HOLES

TOOL FOR MARKING DOWEL HOLES

On some work it is quite difficult to locate the exact point for a dowel, but with the tool illustrated placed between the joint to be made and the parts gently pressed together you have the exact point for the dowel in each piece. The tool is made from a piece of sheet steel about 1/2 in. square with a pin having a point on both ends driven in the center, as shown in Fig. 1. The tool is placed between the pieces that are to be joined, as shown in Fig. 2. The small pin will mark the point for the bit in both pieces exactly opposite.

A MAGAZINE TABLE

This little magazine table will be found a very useful piece of furniture for the den or library. Its small size permits it to be set anywhere in a room without being in the way. Quarter-sawed oak should be used in its construction, and the following pieces will be needed:

4 legs, 2 by 2 by 29 in., S-4-S. 4 end slats, 1/2 by 2 by 10 in., S-4-S. 1 shelf, 1 by 16 by 30 in., S-1-S. 1 top board, 1 by 18 by 36 in., S-1-S.

If you are convenient to a planing mill you can secure these pieces ready cut to length, squared and sanded. This will save you considerable labor.

The four legs are finished on all sides and chamfered at the bottom to prevent the corners from splitting. The mortises for the shelf should be cut 9 in. from the top of each leg, as shown in the sketch. Care should be taken to make these a perfect fit.

The shelf should be finished on the top side and the four edges, and the corners cut out to fit the mortises in the table legs. An enlarged view of this joint is shown in the sketch.

The top board may have to be made of two 9-in. boards, dove-tailed and glued together. It should be finished on the top side and the edges. The edges can be beveled if desired. The board is fastened to the legs by means of screws through four small brass angles. These angles can be made or they can be purchased at any hardware store.

The top board and the shelf should be mortised at each end for the 1/2 by 2-in. slats. These slats should be finished on all sides.

The table is now ready to be assembled and glued together. The glue should dry at least 24 hours before the clamps are removed.

After the glue is dry, carefully go over the entire table with fine sandpaper and remove all surplus glue and rough spots. It can now be finished in any one of the mission stains which are supplied by the trade for this purpose.

A WASTE PAPER BASKET

A waste paper basket of pleasing design, and very easy to construct, is shown in the accompanying sketch. Quarter-sawed oak is the best wood to use, and it is also the easiest to obtain. The following pieces will be needed:

1 bottom piece, 3/4 by 9 in. square.
4 corner pieces, 3/4 in. square by 15-1/2 in.
4 top rails, 3/4 in. square by 7-1/2 in.
12 slats, 1/4 by 3/4 by 16-1/4 in.
4 blocks, 1 in. square.
4 F.H. screws, 2-1/2 in. long.
24 R.H. screws, 3/4 in. long.

If the pieces are ordered from the mill cut to length, squared and sanded, much labor will be saved. First bevel the ends of the corner posts and the slats, as shown, and finish them with sandpaper. Bore the holes in the posts and the railing for the dowel pins. These pins should be about 3/8 in. in diameter and 3/4 in. long. When this is done the parts can be glued together and laid aside to dry. The four blocks 1 in. square are for the feet. Bore holes through these blocks and the corners of the bottom board for the large screws to go through. Fasten them together by running the screws through the blocks, and the board into the ends of the corner posts as shown in the sketch. The 1/4-in. slats can now be fastened on with the small round-headed screws. They should be evenly spaced on the four sides. This completes the basket except for the finish. This can be any one of the many finishes supplied by the trade for this purpose.

AN OAK WRITING DESK

For the writing desk shown in the accompanying picture the following stock will be needed. The thicknesses of all the pieces are specified. On the legs the widths, too, are specified. Quarter-sawed white oak is the best wood to use, and it should be well seasoned and clear of shakes and other imperfections.

Stock Bill

2 front posts, 1-5/8 by 1-5/8 by 34 in., S-4-S., oak.
2 back posts, 1-5/8 by 1-5/8 by 42 in., S-4-S., oak.
2 lower side rails, 3/4 by 3-1/4 by 15 in., S-2-S., oak.
1 lower back rail, 3/4 by 3-1/4 by 27 in., S-2-S., oak.
2 sides, 3/4 by 9 by 14 in., S-2-S., oak.
2 sides, 3/4 by 10-1/2 by 14 in., S-2-S., oak.
1 back, 3/4 by 9 by 26 in., S-2-S., oak.
1 back, 3/4 by 10-1/2 by 26 in., S-2-S., oak.
1 top, 3/4 by 6 by 30-in., S-2-S., oak.
1 lid, 3/4 by 15 by 28 in., S-2-S., oak.
2 side shelves, 3/4 by 5 by 16 in., S-2-S., oak.
4 braces, 3/4 by 1-1/4 by 9 in., S-2-S., oak.
1 bottom of case, 3/4 by 16 by 28 in., S-2-S., oak.

Interior

1 piece, 3/4 by 16 by 27 in., S-2-S., oak.
4 drawer and case bottom supports, 3/4 by 2-1/2 by 28 in., S-2-S., oak.
6 drawer and case bottom supports, 3/4 by 2-1/2 by 16 in., S-2-S., oak.
4 drawer guides, 3/4 by 3/4 by 16 in., S-2-S., oak.

Drawers

2 front pieces, 3/4 by 7-1/2 by 13 in., S-2-S., oak.
4 side pieces, 3/8 by 7-1/2 by 16 in., S-2-S., poplar.
2 back pieces, 3/8 by 7 by 12 in., S-2-S., poplar.
2 bottom pieces, 3/8 by 16 by 12 in., S-2-S., poplar.

Pigeon Holes

1 bottom, 3/16 by 7-1/4 by 27 in., S-2-S., poplar.
1 top, 3/16 by 4-1/2 by 27 in., S-2-S., poplar.
4 verticals, 3/16 by 7-1/4 by 10 in., S-2-S., poplar.
1 vertical, 3/16 by 4-1/2 by 4 in., S-2-S., poplar.
5 horizontals, 3/16 by 7-1/2 by 9 in., S-2-S., poplar.
2 horizontals, 4-1/2 by 9 in., S-2-S., poplar.

Drawers In Pigeon Holes

2 front, 3/8 by 2-1/4 by 9 in., S-2-S., poplar.
4 sides, 3/16 by 2-1/4 by 7-1/4 in., S-2-S., poplar.
2 backs, 3/16 by 2-1/4 by 9 in., S-2-S., poplar.
2 bottoms, 3/16 by 7-1/4 by 9 in., S-2-S., poplar.

Begin work by cutting the posts to length and shape. Having done this, lay out the tenons on the lower rails so as to have the required distances between the shoulders, and then cut them. Now cut the parts to be worked into the frames that support the drawer and bottom of the case, and glue them properly. While this is drying, the other parts of the case may be laid out and shaped. It is intended that the sides of the case shall splice on the edge of the bottom of the pigeon hole case. In this manner the side shelves will cover the joint on either end. The back may be made up into one solid piece. Make the side pieces of the case long enough to be housed into the posts about 3/8 in. at each end.

The shelves at the ends of the desk should be fastened after the frame is put together and before the bottom of the case for the pigeon holes is fitted and fastened. In so doing the shelves may be fastened from the inside of the case. The angles of the braces are 30-60 deg. It will be noted that the edges of the lid are rabbeted. Another way is to have the lid large enough to fit entirely over the sides of the case and change the slope to correspond.

The drawers may be made next. The fronts should be of oak, but the other parts of yellow poplar. An examination of an ordinary drawer will show the manner of construction.

Make the frame of the pigeon holes of 3/16-in. yellow poplar. The drawing shows an arrangement entirely independent of the sides of the desk so that the frame can be made and slipped in place after the finish has been put on. Two drawers are shown. These are faced front and back alike so as to secure as much room in the drawer as possible.

In the finishing, the poplar wood should be finished with white shellac in the natural light color of the wood. For the oak parts the following is appropriate for this design: Apply one coat of green Flemish water stain. When this has dried, sandpaper lightly until the raised grain has been removed, and apply another coat of stain diluted one-half with water. When dry, sand lightly and apply a very thin coat of shellac. Sand lightly and apply a coat of dark filler, natural filler colored with lamp-black, according to the somberness of the finish desired. Upon this put a coat of orange shellac. After this, put on two coats of a good rubbing varnish. Rub the first coats with curled hair or haircloth and the last with pulverized pumice stone and raw linseed oil or crude oil.

AN OAK COUCH WITH CUSHIONS

This beautiful piece of mission furniture can be made at a very moderate cost, if the material used for the cushions is of good imitation leather. These substitutes for leather last fully as long and the difference can only be detected by an expert. White oak will give the best results except for the frames or slats on which the cushions rest and these may be made of poplar or pine. If a mill or woodworking shop of any kind is handy, the hardest part of the work can be saved by securing the following list of material, cut, planed, sanded and squared up to the exact sizes given:

2 posts, 3 in. square by 17 in.
2 posts, 3 in. square by 26 in.
2 rails, 7/8 by 8 by 82 in.
1 rail, 7/8 by 8 by 25 in.
1 end, 7/8 by 18 by 25 in.
1 piece, 7/8 by 9 by 24-1/2 in.

The last piece on the list when sawed diagonal makes the two slanting pieces at the head of the couch. The corner braces are made from two pieces of straight-grained oak, 2 by 4-1/2 by 4-1/2 in., sawed on the diagonal, and cut as shown in the enlarged plan section to make the four pieces.

First be sure the legs are perfectly square, the two short ones and the two long ones of equal length respectively. Either chamfer or round the upper ends as desired, chisel and plane the taper on the lower ends. Lay out and cut all the tenons on the rails—1 in. is the amount allowed at each end in the stock dimensions given. Arrange the posts and rails in the positions they are to occupy in the finished couch. Number each tenon and the place its corresponding mortise is to be cut in the post. Mark each mortise directly from the tenon which is to fit into it, taking care to have all the rails an equal distance from the floor. Bore and chisel out all mortises and see that all the rails fit perfectly, before proceeding with the work.

The next step will be to fit in the slanting side pieces at the head of the couch. These must be let into the long posts 1/2 in. and held also by a dowel in the side rail. In order to get these pieces into place, the mortise in the long post must be made 1/2 in. longer than the tenon on the sloping side piece so the tenon may be first pushed into the mortise and then the side clamped down on the rail over the dowel. The whole couch should fit together perfectly before gluing any of the parts.

Glue the end parts together first. Hot glue will hold best if the room and lumber are warm; if these cannot be had, use cold glue. After the ends have set for at least 24 hours, glue in place the side rails and slanting head pieces. Screw in place the corner braces. Be sure when making these braces to have the grain running diagonally across the corner, or the brace will be weak, also, be sure the sides are square with the ends; this may be determined by measuring the diagonals to find if they are equal.

If it is decided to use frames for the cushions, then the following material will be necessary:

2 pieces, 7/8 by 2 by 56 in.

2 pieces, 7/8 by 2 by 25 in.

4 pieces 7/8 by 2 by 21 in.

This material may be of pine or poplar. These pieces are made into two frames as shown in the drawing and held together with long screws or nails. Fasten with glue and screw short blocks on the inside of the couch rails for holding the two frames in place. Tack pieces of cheap burlap across the frame and cover with ordinary black cambric. This will give a strong, springy rest for the cushions.

Should slats be used instead of frames for holding the cushions, then the following list of material should be substituted for the frame material list:

2 cleats, 7/8 by 2 by 56 in.

2 cleats, 7/8 by 2 by 25 in.

12 slats, 3/4 by 5 by 25 in.

The materials listed may be of soft wood the same as for the frame. The cleats are fastened to the inside of the rails of the couch with screws, so the top edge will be 2 in. lower than the top edge of the rails. The slats are spaced evenly on these cleats.

After the glue is all set, remove the clamps and scrape off any glue that may be on the wood. If this glue is not removed it will keep the stain from entering the wood, which will show up when finished in white spots.

This couch may be stained in any of the shades of brown or dark to harmonize with its lines of construction. A water stain will penetrate the wood best and after this is applied and thoroughly dried the surface should be well sanded to remove the roughness of the raised grain. Apply one coat of thin shellac and when this is dry, put on two coats of wax.

In making up the cushions, use either hair or elastic felt for the filling.

ELECTRIC SHADE FOR THE DINING ROOM

The dining shade shown is constructed of wood and glass. There will be needed the following:

8 pieces, 3/4 by 3/4 by 24 in., S-4-S, oak.

4 pieces, 3/4 by 3/4 by 4 in., S-4-S, oak.

4 pieces, 3/4 by 3/4 by 10-1/2 in., S-4-S, oak.

4 pieces, 3/8 by 3/4 by 23 in., S-4-S, oak.

8 pieces, 3/8 by 3/4 by 10 in., S-4-S, oak.

4 pieces, 3/8 by 3/4 by 9 in., S-4-S, oak.

1 piece, 3/4 by 8 by 8 in., S-4-S, oak.

Begin work by shaping the ends of the longest pieces as shown in the drawing. All the angles are 45 deg. Next lay out the cross-lap joints at the corners so that two sets of horizontal frames shall be formed 23 by 23 in. Cut four pieces to a length of 3 in. each. Also shape up the "false" extensions of these pieces which are to be fastened below the lower frame at the corners. Since these are to be cut from the pieces just specified, the easiest way is to shape the end of each to the required angle and then crosscut. Rabbet these pieces sufficient to allow the art glass to set in on the back sides and be fastened—about 1/4 in. will do—and put them together with glue and brads.

Now make the top square in a similar manner, except the rabbets. In this top square is to be fitted the 3/4-in. board which is to hold the lights and to which the chains are to be fastened.

The sloping sides are next to be made. The sides are to be built up separately, the corners being lapped and glued after rabbeting the under arrises sufficient to let the glass in. The four sides are mitered together at their edges and reinforced by covering the joint with copper.

These sides are next mitered to the top and bottom frames and made fast on the under sides with copper strips, glue being used on the edges of the wood.

The shade shown had a mottled glass in which greens predominated. The sizes and shapes of these pieces of glass would better be determined after the woodwork is finished.

One manner of fastening the chains is clearly shown in the photograph. Such a combination will call for an extra piece of oak, 3/4 by 3-1/4 by 3-1/4 in. finished stock.

A good finish for this shade is obtained as follows: Put on a coat of silver gray water stain. When this has dried, sand lightly with No. 00 sandpaper and apply a coat of golden oak oil stain. Allow this to dry after wiping the surplus off with a cloth. Put on a coat of black paste filler and allow to harden over night. When dry, sand lightly and put on a coat of very thin shellac. Sand this lightly when hard and put on a coat of wax. This is a very dark finish relieved by high lights of lighter brown and is known as Antwerp oak.

PART III. HOW TO BEND WOOD

HOW TO BEND WOOD

The process for making bent wood for furniture parts is the same as for any other kind of bent-wood work. The pieces should be made close to the size, with only enough material left on them for "cleaning up" after the bending has been done. The pieces used for the bent work should be good, clean, "live" lumber. Lumber dried on the stump will not bend.

A box must be made in which to steam the pieces of wood to be bent. A design of a steaming box is shown in the illustration. Such a box is made by nailing four boards together into a square or rectangular form, the boards having a length sufficient to take in the length of the furniture parts to be bent. Both ends of the finished box are squared up and closed with a board cut to the size, using felt or gunny sack in the joint to make it as tight as possible. These ends can be nailed on, but it is best to hold them with a bar of metal set against each one. Nailing the ends a few times would spoil the box for further use in steaming.

A good teakettle will serve the purpose for a steam generator. A hose is attached to the spout of the teakettle, as shown in the illustration, and to the steaming box in a like manner. The steaming box should be provided with a short piece of gas pipe turned into a hole bored into one of the sides used for the top on which to attach the hose. A small hole should be bored into one side of one end of the steaming box, and this end should be arranged a trifle lower than the other end. The hole will permit the water of condensation to escape. Steam should not escape from the box when a charge of wood is being softened. Steam which escapes from the box in the form of vapor has done no work whatever, and is just so much waste of fuel. In order to give up its heat to the wood, the steam must condense and come away from the box as water. Therefore, in steaming a charge of pieces in the box, never crowd the teakettle so hard that the steam escapes around the heads of the box or through any other joints. The steam should be supplied to the box just as fast as it condenses, and no faster. When the pieces are placed in the box they should be so arranged that the steam can find ready access to all sides of each piece.

The curve or bend of the piece to be made must be marked out on a wide board or on the floor. Nail down several blocks of wood or pieces cut out like brackets on the board or floor against the drawing, as shown in the illustration. The wood is sprung between these blocks or forms after it has been softened by steam. When taking the steamed pieces from the box do not lose any time in securing them to the forms. Do not take out more than one piece at a time, as it must be bent to the forms immediately after taking it from the hot steam. The time of the steaming will vary with the size of the pieces. Small strips may be steamed in 15 or 20 minutes, while large ones may require several hours to become soft enough to bend. The pieces must be left in the forms until they are thoroughly dry.

A SMOKING STAND

When making the smoking stand shown in the accompanying photograph, use quarter-sawed oak, if possible, as this wood is the most suitable for finishing in the different mission stains. This little piece of furniture is very attractive, easy to construct, and is an article that a smoker would appreciate.

If the stock is purchased finished and sandpapered, it will save much of the hard work. The material needed is as follows:

One piece, 7/8 by 12 in. by 9 ft. long, for the legs.
One piece, 7/8 by 10 in. by 4 ft. long, for the top.
One piece, 7/8 by 8 in. by 1 ft. long, for the shelves.
One piece, 1/2 by 2 in. by 6 ft. long, for the pipe rack.

The legs can be made first. Cut four pieces off the 12-in. board, each exactly 25 in. long, and lay each one out with a pair of compasses as shown in the detail drawing at Fig. 1. With a circle or keyhole saw cut out the piece, then shave out the saw marks and sandpaper smooth.

Next take the 8-in. board and make the shelves. Set a bevel protractor at a 45-deg. angle, lay out the pieces as shown in Fig. 5, and cut them out with a saw. Eight pieces are cut out as shown in Fig. 4. These pieces can be cut out of the scraps left from cutting the legs and shelves. Cut them so that the grain runs the long way. Place two of these braces on the bench with the beveled ends toward each other, but with a piece of 7/8-in. stock between them, and the other two beveled ends resting against a straightedge. Fasten them to the bench with a couple of nails, leaving the heads sticking up so that you can pull them later with a claw hammer. Remove the straightedge and slide the piece that is between the braces along until it projects 4 or 5 in. from the side formed by the straightedge. Then place two more braces in the corners formed by this piece, put two 7/8-in. pieces between the two braces that are fastened, and the two that are loose, so that each brace will be in its proper place. Fasten the last two the same as the first pair. Then remove all the pieces from between the braces and place the tops of the legs in their stead. These should be fastened to the braces with 1-in. screws of small diameter, put in at an angle. Bore a hole in straight for about 1/4-in. with a 1/4-in. bit for each screw, and then run a gimlet at an angle into the leg. After you have the legs fastened to the first set of braces, measure up from the bench 10 in. and put in another set, being careful to get them all the same distance from the bench, as the inner corners of the shelves rest on these braces. Now pull out the nails and set the stand on its feet.

Next put in the shelves. Place the inner corner of one on one of the braces, and fasten it there with a screw put through the brace from the bottom. Now fasten a clamp on each leg at the ends of the shelf in such a manner as to form a support on the top side of the shelf. Then put four screws through the shelf from the bottom into the legs. Repeat the operation on each shelf, being careful to get them all the same height. Four pieces like Fig. 3 should now be made. These pieces will have to be fitted in place as they should slant outward so that it will be easy to put articles through the holes. The holes should be about 5/8-in. diameter.

The top can be made by cutting off two pieces from the 10-in. board, each 20 in. long, and fastening them together with dowels. Smooth the ends and be sure that the boards match evenly. It makes a better job to glue the top together, in addition to the dowels, and, if you do this, it would be better to make the top first. Then it will have time to dry before you are ready to use it. In putting on the top, care should be taken to get each of the corners an equal distance from the legs. Then a screw may be put up through each one of the braces and two or three through each leg into the top. Now smooth all rough and uneven places with fine sandpaper and apply the finish. Secure some metal matchsafes and scratchers, fasten on as shown in the photograph, and the stand is complete.

A CHINA CLOSET

This beautiful piece of mission furniture can be made by anyone who has a few good tools and knows how to use them. The cost is very moderate and if you are convenient to a mill a great amount of labor can be saved by ordering the pieces ready cut to length, squared, and sanded. Quarter-sawed oak should be used and the material needed will be as follows:

4 posts, 2 by 2 by 54 in., S-4-S.

2 top and bottom boards, 3/4 by 15-3/4 by 39-1/2 in., S-1-S.
2 shelves, 3/4 by 15-1/2 by 38 in., S-2-S.
2 lower end braces, 3/4 by 5 by 15 in., S-2-S.
2 upper end braces, 3/4 by 4-1/4 by 15 in., S-2-S.
1 lower front board, 3/4 by 3 by 40 in., S-1-S.
1 upper front board, 3/4 by 2-1/4 by 40 in., S-1-S.
4 door frames, 3/4 by 1-3/4 by 43-1/2 in., S-2-S.
4 door frames, 3/4 by 2 by 19 in., S-2-S.
4 upright end pieces, 3/4 by 1-1/2 by 39-1/2 in., S-2-S.
5 back pieces, 1/2 by 8 by 46-1/2 in., S-1-S.
2 cleats, 1 by 1 by 37-3/4 in., soft wood.
4 cleats, 1 by 1 by 12-3/4 in., soft wood.
4 blocks, 1/2 by 1 by 1-1/2 in.

First be sure the posts are perfectly square and of equal length. Either chamfer or round the upper ends as desired. The mortises can be laid out and cut, or they can be left until the tenons are all made and then marked and cut directly from each tenon.

The top and bottom boards should have the corners cut to clear the posts as shown in the drawing. The top board should be finished on both sides and the bottom one on the upper side only and be sure to get the best side up.

Cut the tenons on the front boards back 1/4 in. from the face as shown in the end view. The boards should be finished on the outside sides and edges. The end pieces are fitted and finished in a similar manner except that the inside edge is rabbeted for the glass as shown. The side pieces are also rabbeted for the glass and the posts have grooves 1/2 in. deep cut in them to hold these side pieces. They are glued in place and this can be done after the frame is put together.

The two shelves are finished on both sides and the front edges. The doors are fitted in the usual manner by a tenon and mortise joint at the ends. They are rabbeted on the inside for the glass and are finished on all sides.

Before gluing any of the parts together, see that they all fit and go together perfectly square. The posts, side, and front pieces should be glued and assembled, then the top and bottom boards put in place to hold the frame square when the clamps are put on. Leave dry for about 24 hours, then scrape all the surplus glue from about the joints as the finish will not take when there is any glue. Fasten the top and bottom boards to the frame by means of screws through cleats as shown in the drawing. The backing is put on and finished on the front side. A mirror can be put in the back without much trouble, if it is desired. The shelves should be put in place and held at the back by screws through the backing and at the front by two small blocks on the posts as shown.

After the closet is all assembled it should be thoroughly gone over with fine sandpaper before any finish is applied. It can be finished in any one of the many mission stains which are supplied by the trade for this purpose.

A LEATHER COVERED FOOTSTOOL

The illustration shows a very handy footstool in mission style. The following list of materials will be needed:

4 oak posts, 1-1/2 by 1-1/2 by 12 in., S-4-S.
2 sides, 3/4 by 3 by 12 in., soft wood.
2 ends, 3/4 by 3 by 8 in., soft wood.
1 bottom, 3/4 by 8 by 12 in., soft wood.
1 small box of 8 oz. tacks
2-1/2 doz. ornamental head nails.
1 piece of dark leather, 16 by 20 in.
1/2 lb. hair and a small portion of mission stain.

The posts are the only parts made of quarter-sawed oak, the other parts, being covered with leather, can be made of any kind of soft wood. Chamfer the top end of each post, and taper the lower ends as shown in detail. When this is done the mortises can be cut for the sides as shown in the post detail. When cutting the mortises and tenons take care to make them fit perfectly, as there is nothing to brace the legs at the bottom. The strength of the stool depends upon the joints. Make the surface of the posts smooth by first using No. 1 sandpaper, then finishing with No. 00.

The parts are now assembled. First clamp the ends together, using plenty of glue on the joints, and drive some small nails on the inside of the posts through the tenon ends. When the glue has set, the remaining sides can be put together the same as the ends. Fit the bottom on the inside about 1 in. from the top. This can be made fast by driving nails through the sides and ends of the board. The finishing is done by putting on the mission stain as the directions state on the can, then wax the surface to get a dull gloss.

The leather is now put on. Notch out the corners to fit around the posts, but do not cut the ends off. Lap them under the cover. Before nailing on the cover fix the hair evenly over the top, about 6 in. deep. Draw the leather over the hair and fasten the edges with the 8-oz. tacks. The ornamental nails are driven in last, as shown in the drawing, to make a good appearance.

ARTS CRAFTS MANTEL CLOCK

The clock shown in the illustration was designed especially for rooms furnished in mission style. The clock, however, may be made of mahogany or other wood to match the furniture in any room where it is to be placed. If the mission effect is desired, an oxidized or copper sash should be used. Movements can be bought at the salesroom of a clock company. A movement should be selected that is wide enough from the front to the back to allow the clock case to be made sufficiently deep for standing without being easily upset.

Quarter-sawed white oak is the best material for this clock, but any other wood which works easily and takes a stain well may be used. Two pieces, 3/8 in. thick, 6-1/2 in. wide, and 8-1/2 in. long, will be needed for the front and back. One piece, 5 in. wide, 6 in. long, and with a thickness sufficient for the clock movement, is needed for the middle part. The thickness of this piece depends on the movement secured.

After the front and back pieces are finished, and a piece of hammered copper screwed on the front as shown in the drawing, the middle piece must be made just thick enough to make the whole distance from the front of the copper to the back of the clock equal to the depth of the movement. Plane one edge on both front and back pieces. Lay out the design and the centers for the circular holes from this planed edge. Use a plane and chisel to cut the outside design. The hole can be bored out with an expansive bit, or sawed out with a scroll saw, and filed perfectly round with a half-round wood file. The bit will give the best results. If the bit is used, bore holes in a piece of scrap wood until the exact size is found.

The outside design of the piece of copper is made to correspond to the design of the clock. The circular hole in the copper can be cut with the expansive bit by first punching a hole in the center to receive the spur of the bit, placing on a block of wood and boring through a little way. The spur on the cutter will cut out the copper. Fasten the copper to the front with copper nails or round-headed screws.

If good glue can be had, the three pieces of wood may be glued together. If the glue cannot be relied upon, put in two flat-headed screws from the back.

The clock can be finished with a dark stain and waxed, or, as it is small, it can be easily fumed. If stain is used, stain and wax the pieces before putting them together. The fuming process is more easily done after the clock is assembled. Secure a bucket, a peck measure, or any receptacle large enough, when inverted, to put over the clock. Pour about 2 oz. of strong ammonia into a saucer or small pan. Support the clock above the saucer and cover both with the inverted bucket. Allow it to stand for three or four days—the longer it stands the darker the fumed finish will be. Finish with two coats of bleached wax. Do not use ordinary uncolored wax, as it will show in the unfilled pores of the wood. The works of the clock should not be in the frame while fuming.

A MUSIC STAND

The attractive and useful piece of mission furniture shown in the accompanying illustration is made of quarter-sawed oak. Considerable labor can be saved in its construction if the stock is ordered from the mill ready cut to length, squared and sanded. The stock list consists of the following pieces:

1 top, 3/4 by 16 by 20 in., S-2-S.
1 shelf, 3/4 by 11-1/2 by 15 in., S-2-S.
1 shelf, 3/4 by 12 by 15 in., S-2-S.
1 shelf, 3/4 by 14-1/2 by 15 in., S-2-S.
1 shelf, 3/4 by 16 by 15 in., S-1-S.
4 legs, 3/4 by 5 by 41 in., S-2-S.
2 lower crosspieces, 3/4 by 3 by 9 in., S-2-S.
2 upper crosspieces, 3/4 by 2 by 9 in., S-2-S.
4 end slats, 5/8 by 2 by 34 in., S-2-S.
20 R.H. screws, 2 in. long.

The four shelves and the top are so wide that it will be necessary to make them from two or more pieces glued together. The top should have a 1/4-in. bevel cut around the upper edge as shown in the drawing.

The curve of the legs can be cut with a bracket saw or a drawknife, care being taken to get the edges square and smooth. The four crosspieces are fastened to the legs by means of tenons and mortises. The end slats are joined to the crosspieces in the same manner. The legs can be assembled in pairs with the slats and crosspieces in place. They can be glued in this position, and when dry they should be carefully gone over with fine sandpaper to remove all rough spots. The shelves can now be put in place. They should be fastened to the legs with round-headed screws. The top is also fastened on with screws. When applying the finish, remove the top board and the shelves and finish them separately. The stand can be finished in any one of the many mission stains supplied by the trade for this purpose.

This handsome piece of furniture can be used as a magazine stand as well as a music stand, if desired, and, if it is made and finished well, it will prove an ornament to any home.

PART IV. MAKING SCREWS HOLD IN END GRAIN

MAKING SCREWS HOLD IN END GRAIN

It is often necessary to fasten one piece of wood to the end of another by means of screws. Wood being a fibrous material, it can be readily understood that when a screw having sharp threads is put in the end grain parallel to these fibers the threads cut them in such a way that, when an extra strain is put upon the parts, the screw pulls out, bringing with it the severed fibers. The accompanying sketch shows how this difficulty may be overcome, and at the same time make the screw hold firmly. A hole is bored and a dowel, preferably of hardwood, glued in it, the grain at right angles to that of the piece.

The size of the dowel, and its location, can be determined by the diameter and the length of the screw. The dowel need not extend all the way through the piece, but should be put in from the surface where the grain of the dowel will be least objectionable.

When putting screws in hard wood much labor will be saved by applying soap to the threads.

A WALL CASE WITH A MIRROR DOOR

The wall case shown in the accompanying picture will serve well as a medicine case. Having a paneled door in which is set a mirror, it serves equally well as a shaving case. It is best made of some hard wood, though a soft wood such as pine or yellow poplar will work up easier and look well finished with three or four coats of white enamel paint.

There will be needed the following pieces:

2 sides, 5/8 by 6 by 32-1/2 in., S-4-S.

1 top and 1 bottom, 5/8 by 6 by 18 in., S-4-S.

1 top of back, 1/2 by 4 by 16-1/4 in., S-2-S.
1 bottom of back, 1/2 by 3 by 16-1/4 in., S-4-S.
1 shelf, 5/8 by 5 by 16 in., S-4-S.
1 back, 1/4 by 16 by 21 in., S-2-S.

Door

2 stiles, 5/8 by 3 by 20-1/2 in., S-4-S.
1 top rail, 5/8 by 2 by 11 in., S-4-S.
1 bottom rail, 5/8 by 4 by 11 in., S-4-S.
1 backing for door, 3/16 by 10 by 15 in., S-2-S.

First shape the ends of the two side pieces as shown in the drawing. Next square the top and bottom pieces of the case to size, and lay out and cut the tenons on the ends. Lay out and cut the mortises in the side pieces, also the groove for the shelf, having first squared the shelf to size. Cut and shape the top and bottom pieces of the back as shown. Cut the rebates in the side pieces into which these pieces are to rest their ends. Cut the rebate for the back. Thoroughly scrape and sandpaper these parts and assemble them. Cut and fit the back in place.

The door is to be made next. Plan the different parts of the door so that the edges may be planed to fit the opening; that is, make the door a good quarter larger at top and bottom than the opening. In cutting the rebate the easiest way is to use a rabbeting plane and cut the full length of the pieces. By using a tenon on the rails in which one shoulder is as much longer than the other as the rebate is deep there is no resulting groove showing at the corner.

The wood should be finished before the glass is set, at least, it should be filled, if of hard wood, and one coat of paint put on, if of soft wood which is to be enameled.

In setting the glass, place a thin cushion of putty between the rebate and the glass and another thin cushion between the glass and the fillet of wood or the backing which is to protect the back of the glass.

Fit the door, and then put on the hinges and lock. If desired, the tenons may be made keyed as shown in the photograph instead of through as shown in the drawing.

To finish the case, if of oak, apply a coat of light paste filler, the directions being on the filler can. Next put on a coat of white shellac. When this has hardened apply two coats of some good varnish. Allow time for each coat to harden and rub the first coats with haircloth or curled hair, and the last with pulverized pumice and raw linseed oil or crude oil.

If the wood is soft and an enamel white is desired, the enamel is applied not unlike paint. The directions will be found on the cans in which the paint is purchased.

A SIDE CHAIR

A side chair of simple design and construction is here given. The great difficulty with most chair designs is that the back is generally designed narrower than the front, thus necessitating the rails entering the posts or legs at angles. To the amateur this is quite confusing. The chair illustrated is the same in width, both back and front, so that the shoulders of all the rails are at right angles to the sides. The back of the chair is straight, thus simplifying the design still more.

Another thing which is confusing to the beginner in his efforts to lay out the mortises is the irregular placing of the rails. It will be noted that in this design the rails of side, front and back are on the same level.

Plain sawed red oak will be appropriate for this piece. Have the pieces mill-planed and sandpapered on four sides to size, allowing 1/2 in. extra to the lengths for squaring up the ends.

There will be needed the following:

4 rails, 7/8 by 2 by 17-1/2 in.
4 rails, 3/4 by 2 by 17-1/2 in.
2 front posts, 1-1/2 by 1-1/2 by 19 in.
2 rear posts, 1-1/2 by 1-1/2 by 37-1/2 in.
1 back, 3/4 by 9-3/4 by 17-1/2 in.
2 cleats, 3/8 by 1 by 16 in.
4 slats, 3/8 by 2 by 16-1/2 in.

Begin work by cutting the posts to the lengths indicated in the drawing. The lower ends should be chamfered slightly to prevent their splintering from usage. The top ends are cut to an angle of 45 deg., the slope beginning 1/2 in. below the top. Lay out and cut the mortises. To do this, lay off the measurements on one of the posts, then place all four side by side on the bench, with the face marks up. Even the ends with the try-square and then carry the measurements just made across all of them, using the try-square. The rails ought to be shouldered on all four sides. Three-eighths inch is a good thickness for the tenons. The width may be 1-1/4 in. and the length 1 in.

Place the rails side by side on the bench with the joint-edges up and the ends evened. Measure off the desired length on one of them and carry the lines across all of them to indicate the location of the shoulder lines. Separate the pieces and square these lines entirely around all of the sides of each piece. With the tenon saw rip and cross cut to these lines.

The back, it will be noted, is set on a slant to add comfort. Thoroughly clean all the parts and assemble them, using good hot glue. Put the back together first, then the front. After these have dried, put the side rails in place.

Cut and fit the two cleats—one to the front rail and one to the rear rail. Keep them even with the lower edge of the rail so as to form a slight recess at the top when the slats are in place. This is to keep the cushion from sliding off. The slats need not be "let into" the cleats but merely fastened to their top edges. The cushion may be made of Spanish roan skin and should be filled with elastic felt.

In the chair shown, the joints are reinforced by the addition of lag screws. If the glue is good and the joints well fitted, these are not necessary.

AN ARM CHAIR

The arm chair here described and illustrated is intended to be one of the set of diners made after the design of the side chair described on another page. The same general directions for making the side chair apply equally to the arm chair.

The stock given in the following list should be purchased surfaced on four sides and well sandpapered:

2 rear posts, 1-1/2 by 1-1/2 by 38 in.

2 front posts, 1-1/2 by 1-1/2 by 26-1/2 in.

9 rails, 7/8 by 2 by 19-1/2 in.

1 rail, 7/8 by 1-1/2 by 19-1/2 in.

3 slats, 1/2 by 2 by 12-1/2 in.

2 arms, 7/8 by 4-1/2 by 20-1/2 in.

2 brackets, 7/8 by 2-1/4 by 2-1/2 in.

2 cleats, 3/8 by 1 by 19 in.

4 slats, 3/8 by 2 by 19 in.

Prepare the posts first by cutting them to the lengths shown in the drawing. In the photograph the front posts have their tops cut off square and the arms fastened to them by means of lag screws. A better way from a mechanical point of view would be to shoulder the top ends on the four sides, cut through-mortises in the arms and insert these tenoned posts into these mortises, pinning the arm to the post by means of small dowels in the edge of the post and through the tenon.

The brackets under the arms are to be fastened to the posts and arms by means of concealed dowels and glue of good quality.

All of the rails should be tenoned into the posts thoroughly, even if the lag screw fastenings are used. If the lag screws are used, the tenons may be what are known as stubb tenons—tenons of short length. Good hot glue should be used in either case.

The shape of the arms is indicated in the drawing. They are fastened to the rear posts by means of dowels and glue.

The slats, or verticals, of the back should not have their ends tenoned but should have the mortises in the rails cut sufficiently large to "let in" the whole end of each. This is much easier and more likely to result in a satisfactory fit than to shoulder them. Any unevenness in the lengths of the respective slats will not affect the fitting of the joints by this latter method.

The tops of the rear posts in this chair, as in the side chair, are cut to angles of 45 deg., beginning the slope at lines marked 1/2 in. from the tops.

The bottom is made up of 2-in. slats fitted between the front and back rails and fastened to cleats which have been previously fastened to the insides of the front and back rails. Keep these cleats low enough on the rails so that the top surfaces of the slats shall rest somewhat below the top edges of the rails. Cushions, such as the one shown, can be purchased ready made or they can be easily made by the amateur.

A good finish for this chair and its mates is obtained as follows: Apply one coat of brown Flemish water stain. This stain in the original package is very dark in tone and unless an almost black finish is wanted, it should be lightened by the addition of one-half or two-thirds water. Apply with a brush or sponge and allow to dry over night. When dry, sandpaper lightly with fine or worn sandpaper to remove the raised grain caused by the water of the stain. Put on a very thin coat of shellac. This is to prevent the "high lights" in close-grained woods from being discolored by the stain in the filler which is to follow. The shellac being very thin does not fill the pores of the wood perceptibly. Next, sand the shellac coat lightly when it has hardened. Apply a coat of paste filler colored considerably darker than the stain to the tone desired for the open grain. If the filler is well stirred and properly applied, one coat ought to be sufficient. If it does not fill the pores satisfactorily, apply another coat when the first has had time to harden. Vandyke brown is used to color the filler, if none but natural color is to be had. On the hardened filler apply a thin coat of shellac. On this apply several coats of wax. The directions for waxing will be found upon the cans in which the wax comes.

A BOOKCASE

This beautiful piece of mission furniture can be made at a very moderate cost by anyone who has a slight knowledge of tools. Considerable labor can be saved by ordering the material from the mill ready cut to size, dressed and sanded. Quarter-sawed oak is the best wood to use and it is comparatively easy to obtain. Plain-sawed oak looks well, but is more liable to warp than the quarter-sawed and this is quite an element in pieces as wide as the ones used. For the complete bookcase the following material will be needed:

1 top, 3/4 by 15 by 31-1/4 in., hard wood, S-1-S.
1 top back board, 3/4 by 4 by 30-1/4 in., hard wood, S-1-S.
2 sides, 3/4 by 14 by 50 in., hard wood, S-1-S.

1 bottom, 3/4 by 14 by 28-3/4 in., hard wood, S-1-S.
1 bottom rail, 3/4 by 4 by 28-3/4 in., hard wood, S-1-S.
1 center piece, 3/4 by 2 by 45-3/4 in., hard wood, S-2-S.
4 door sides, 3/4 by 1-1/2 by 45-1/4 in., hard wood, S-2-S.
4 door ends, 3/4 by 1-1/2 by 14 in., hard wood, S-2-S.
4 pieces door lattice, 1/2 by 1/2 by 12-1/2 in., hard wood.
4 pieces door lattice, 1/2 by 1/2 by 7 in., hard wood.
2 bottom cleats, 1-1/4 by 1-1/4 by 13 in., soft wood.
2 top cleats, 1 by 1 by 12-1/2 in., soft wood.
3 shelves, 1/2 by 12 by 28-1/2 in., soft wood.
12 pieces backing, 3/8 by 4 by 29-3/4 in., soft wood.
4 hinges.
2 door handles.

Begin with the sides by cutting them so they will pair up all right. The front edges are rounded while the back edges are rabbeted on the inside as deep as the backing to be used. The bottoms are cut as shown in the sketch. Holes about 1/2 in. deep should be bored on the inside at the proper places for the wooden pegs which hold up the shelves.

The top and bottom boards should have the front edges rounded and sanded the same as the sides. The top board is sanded on one side only and care should be taken to get the best side up.

Now cut and fit the top back board. This is fastened to the top by means of screws. Screw two cleats to each of the sides as shown and by running screws through these into the top and bottom boards the frame is completed.

The backing which can be made of some cheap lumber is now put on. Next put in the center upright piece between the doors by means of a tenon and mortise at the top and nail at the bottom. The front edge should be rounded and the edge and sides sanded. Cut and fit the bottom rail as shown. It is fastened to the frame by means of cleats on the back side.

The doors are put together by means of a tenon and mortise. They should be rabbeted for the lattice work and the glass. This lattice work can be omitted and leaded glass put in its place which is very becoming to this kind of work.

When the case is completed it must be carefully gone over with sandpaper before any finish is applied.

A mission stain is suitable for work of this kind, but it can also be finished in "golden oak" which is done in the following manner: First put on a golden oak stain and after it has dried for about 2 hours, apply the filler. Let this dry about 10 minutes then rub off with an old rag. Then go over the case again with some very fine sandpaper and after seeing that all parts are free from dust and dirt the varnish can be applied. Three coats of varnish will give a beautiful glossy finish.

A LAMP STAND

A mission table lamp stand for those who use electric lights is shown in the accompanying illustration. It is suitable for either the office or the home and is very simple in design and construction. The stock should be quarter-sawed oak and it can be ordered from the mill ready cut to length, squared and sanded. The following pieces will be needed:

1 post, 1-1/2 in. sq. by 23 in.
1 arm, 1-/8 by 3/4 by 13-1/2 in.
1 block, 3/4 in. thick by 6 in. square.
1 block, 1 in. thick by 9 in. square.

Square up the base blocks and fasten them together with screws as shown in the detail sketch. A mortise, 1 in. square, is cut in the center of the blocks for the center post.. Lead weights, covered with felt, should be attached to the bottom, as shown. The post has a tenon cut on one end to fit the base, and a mortise cut in the other for the arm. Holes are bored in the arm from the ends for the wires. They can be plugged after the wires are in place. A hole is also bored in the top of the center post to connect with the holes in the arm for the lead wire.

It is best to glue the joints together, although this is not necessary if the joints are a tight fit. Sandpaper the parts thoroughly, then stain to match the other furniture.

AN EXTENSION DINING TABLE

The accompanying sketch and photograph show a simple design of an extension dining table of the mission style. It is very easy to construct and can be built at home by anyone who is at all handy with tools. It should be made of quarter-sawed oak, which can be secured at the mill ready cut to length, squared and sanded. Order the following pieces:

2 top pieces, 1 by 23 by 46 in.
2 extra leaves, 1 by 12 by 46 in.
2 rails, 3/4 by 3 by 44 in.
4 rails, 3/4 by 3 by 22 in.
2 pieces for posts, 3/4 by 8 by 24 in.
2 pieces for posts, 3/4 by 6 by 24 in.
4 pieces for feet, 3 by 3 by 14 in.
4 pieces for feet, 3 by 3 by 5 in.
4 pieces for feet, 1 by 4 by 4 in.
4 pieces moulding, 1 by 1 by 10 in.
1 piece, 1 by 12 by 27 in., birchwood.
2 brackets, 3/4 by 3 by 32 in., birchwood.

2 pieces for slide, 1-3/4 by 3 by 36 in., birchwood.

4 pieces for slide, 1 by 3 by 36 in., birchwood.

12 pieces for slide, 3/4 by 1-1/2 by 36 in., birchwood.

The feet can be made first by squaring up one end of each and beveling the other as shown in the drawing. The short pieces are fastened to the long ones by means of long screws and glue. The four square pieces should be nailed to the outer ends and holes bored in them for the casters. Prepare the pieces for the posts, and before nailing them together fasten the feet to them with long screws. Be careful to get them on square, else the table will not set level when complete. Now nail and glue the pieces forming the table together and fasten the moulding at the bottom. This moulding should have mitered corners as shown in the bottom view. Also fasten the rest piece to the top of the post, using long screws and glue.

The slides can be made next. The pieces are made and fastened together with screws as shown in the enlarged detail view. This slide, if made with care, is a good one. The center piece should be firmly fastened to the post rest with long screws. The screws that fasten into the top should be inserted from below through counter-bored holes as shown.

Miter the rails at the corners and glue them to the top. Blocks can be used on the inside if desired, which will make a much stronger construction. Screw the two brackets to the top as shown. These help to support the table when it is extended.

When complete the table should be carefully gone over with fine sandpaper, and all glue and rough spots removed. Apply stain of the desired color. This can be any one of the many mission stains supplied by the trade for this purpose.

PART V. AN OAK BOUND CEDAR CHEST

AN OAK BOUND CEDAR CHEST

This cedar chest for storing unused bedding or furs is not a difficult thing to make and when made, the hard oak binding takes the wear and protects the softer cedar so that the chest ought to serve several generations. Order the stock as follows:

Cedar

2 top and bottom pieces, 7/8 by 16-1/2 by 34-1/2 in., S-2-S.
2 sides, 7/8 by 18-7/8 by 34-1/2 in., S-2-S.
2 ends, 7/8 by 18-7/8 by 14-3/4 in., S-2-S.

Oak

2 overhanging top pieces, 1 by 1 by 36-1/2 in., S-4-S.
2 overhanging top pieces, 1 by 1 by 18-1/2 in., S-4-S.
2 lock and hinge rails, 1 by 2-1/2 by 36-1/2 in., S-2-S.
2 lock and hinge rails, 1 by 2-1/2 by 18-1/2 in., S-2-S.
2 base pieces, 1 by 3-1/4 by 36-1/2 in., S-2-S.
2 base pieces, 1 by 3-1/4 by 18-1/2 in., S-2-S.

Specify thoroughly seasoned Tennessee red cedar and plain sawed white oak and have the different pieces mill-planed and sandpapered as indicated in the stock-bill. This bill allows 1/2 in. extra on the length and the width of each piece for "squaring up" of all pieces except those marked to be surfaced on four sides.

Begin by squaring the sides and ends to size. Probably the best joint for the corners is the dovetail. If the worker is not experienced in woodworking, some of the more simple joints will do. It will be noted that the drawing and stock-bill call for the simplest form of joint, that in which the sides of the chest lap over the end. For the dovetail joint it will be necessary to add 2 in. more to the length of the end pieces, making them 16-3/4 in. each in the rough.

Having got the sides and ends ready, fasten them together. The perspective shows the sides fastened to the ends with ornamental headed nails. Common nails are first used, being equally spaced, and the ornamental heads are afterwards placed so as to cover their heads.

Next square the bottom and nail it to the parts just assembled. Square the top to the same size.

The base stuff is squared on one edge only. The second edge—the upper one—is to be beveled or sloped 1/8 in. to facilitate dusting and for appearance sake. Fit these base pieces to place, mitering the joints. Before fastening the parts to the chest proper, gauge a line 3/4 in. from the lower edge and to a point 4-1/2 in. from each end, cut out to this line and shape the base as shown in the drawing. Use finishing nails for fastening the base to the chest. The heads should be "set" so they may be covered later with a putty colored to match the finish.

In a similar manner plane up, cut and fit the back and hinge rails. These rails should be kept a "scant" 1/8 in. below the top edges of the chest proper. The overhang of the lid fits down over in such a way as to form a dust-proof joint between lid and chest proper.

The overhang of the lid of 1 in. by 1-in. stock may next be mitered, fitted and nailed to the lid. Thoroughly sandpaper all parts not so treated and finish as follows: Put on all the oak pieces, two coats of natural paste filler. This is best done before they are fastened in place. Directions will be found on the cans in which the filler is kept.

The red of the cedar may be heightened by applying a mahogany stain made of Bismark brown aniline and boiling water, in the proportion of 3 qt. of water to 1 oz. of aniline. If applied hot the stain will enter the wood better. When dry, sandpaper lightly with No. 00 paper, both this and the oak-filled pieces.

Fasten the oak pieces in place and give the whole exterior a very thin coat of shellac. After this has hardened, apply two coats of wax. Wax comes in paste form and is to be applied with a cloth very sparingly. Allow it to stand five or ten minutes then rub briskly with a soft dry cloth to polish. The first coat is allowed to stand 24 hours before the second is applied in a similar manner.

Another finish, known as an egg-shell gloss shellac finish, is obtained by omitting the wax and instead applying from two to five more coats of shellac. Allow each coat 24 hours in which to harden, and rub each hardened coat to a smooth finish, using curled hair, or fine steel wool, or fine oiled sandpaper, before applying the next.

The metal reinforcements for the corners can be bought at a hardware store, as can the lock, hinges, and handles. These parts are applied in the usual manner—butt hinges being used.

If well made, the chest is practically airtight. The interior is all of red cedar, while the effect of the exterior in combining the light oak and the red cedar is striking.

A TOOL FOR MAKING MORTISES

In the construction of mission furniture where mortise joints are mostly used, those who cannot have access to a mortising machine will find the following method of great assistance in obtaining a true mortise, which is necessary in work of this kind.

Take a block of wood, A, the exact thickness of the piece B to be mortised, and with an auger bore a hole, the same size as the width of the mortise to be made, exactly parallel to the sides of the block. This can best be done on a drill press or a wood boring machine. If no machine is available, great care should be taken in boring by hand, to get the hole as nearly true as possible. Then nail a cleat, C, on the side of the block, A, and let it extend down on piece B. Use a clamp to hold the block in place while boring out the mortise. By changing the position of the block and boring a number of holes, any length of mortise can be made. The holes should afterwards be squared up with a chisel.

A DRESSER FOR CHILD'S PLAYROOM

This dresser can be made of two kinds of wood as marked on the drawing or it can be made all of one kind. The original dresser was made of oak and walnut and was finished natural, the contrast between the light and dark woods adding much to the value of the piece in the eyes of the little ones. Have all surfaces that will show well sandpapered at the mill. The following is a list of the material wanted:

4 oak posts, 1-1/2 in. square by 19-1/2 in., S-4-S.
3 walnut drawer fronts, 3/4 by 5 by 17 in., S-2-S.
6 yellow poplar drawer sides, 3/8 by 5 by 12 in., S-2-S.
3 yellow poplar backs, 3/8 by 4-1/2 by 16-1/2 in., S-2-S.
3 yellow poplar bottoms, 3/8 by 12 by 16-1/2 in., S-2-S.
4 oak front stretchers, 7/8 by 1-3/4 by 17-1/2 in., S-4-S.
4 oak side rails, 7/8 by 2 by 12 in., S-4-S.
2 walnut side panels, 1/4 by 11 by 14-1/2 in., S-2-S.
8 oak drawer slides, 7/8 by 2 by 10-1/2 in., S-2-S.
6 oak drawer guides, 1/2 by 3/4 by 10-1/2 in., S-2-S.

4 oak back stretchers, 7/8 by 2 by 17-1/2 in., S-2-S.
1 oak top, 5/8 by 14 by 20-1/2 in., S-2-S.
3 sq. ft. of 3/8 in. matched yellow pine ceiling for back.

Mirror Support

1 walnut piece, 7/8 by 1-3/4 by 20-1/2 in., S-2-S.
1 walnut piece, 7/8 by 1-1/2 by 18 in., S-2-S.
1 oak piece, 3/4 by 1-1/4 by 10-1/2 in., S-2-S.
2 oak pieces, 7/8 by 1-1/2 by 11 in., S-2-S.
1 walnut bracket piece, 7/8 by 1-1/4 by 5 in., S-2-S.

Mirror Frame Parts

2 walnut pieces, 7/8 by 1-1/2 by 12-1/2 in., S-2-S.
2 walnut pieces, 7/8 by 1-1/2 by 10-1/2 in., S-2-S.
2 oak pieces, 1/4 by 3/8 by 10 in., S-4-S.
2 oak pieces, 1/4 by 3/8 by 8 in., S-4-S.
1 back, 3/16 by 8 by 10 in., soft wood.
2 cleats, 3/8 by 1-1/4 by 8 in.
1 plain mirror glass, 7-1/2 by 9-1/2 in.

Begin by planing the four posts to length. The lower ends should be slightly beveled to prevent their slivering. Cut the mortises for the tenons that are on the ends of the side rails. These rails are to be 7/8 by 2 in. and the tenons should be 3/8 by 1-1/4 in. wide by 3/4 in. long. The posts should be rabbeted down to their middles to a depth of 3/8 in. so as to receive the 1/4-in. end panels. The end rails should be cut to length and their tenons worked after one edge of each has been rabbeted as were the posts.

Having squared the panels to size, put the two ends of the dresser together with glue. Next make the four frames which are to carry the drawers. They should measure from outside to outside, in length 17-1/2 in.; in width, 12-1/2 in. It is intended that the short pieces shall be tenoned into the long ones. When these frames are ready, cut out each corner as indicated in the cross section drawing. Reduce to size the drawer guides and fasten them in place. Dowel the frames to the ends of the dresser in the places indicated on the drawing. Put on the back, nailing into frames to the ends of the dresser in the places indicated and fasten the top in place, putting screws into it from the under side.

The mirror frame and support should next be made. The drawing shows quite clearly the parts and their relation to each other. All the slopes are of 45 deg. Instead of rabbeting the mirror frame, a 1/4 by 3/8-in. fillet of oak is nailed around to form the recess, the walnut frame and oak fillet making a pretty contrast. All nail holes are to be filled with putty colored to match the finish. Wooden pins or round-head screws are to be used to fasten the mirror frame to its support and should be placed above center an inch or so.

The drawers are to be constructed in the usual manner. It is a good plan to make the grooves 1/16 in. narrower than the stock is thick to insure a fit, chamfering the under or back sides of the bottom and back if necessary. Make the sides of the drawers of such a length that when the drawer has been pushed in as far as it will go, the front will be recessed about 1/4 in. behind the front crosspieces. Groove the inside of the drawer front 3/16 in. to receive the bottom. The mirror should not be placed until the wood has been finished.

Finish the wood natural, apply three coats of varnish. Rub the first two with haircloth or curled hair and the last with pulverized pumice stone and crude oil or raw linseed oil. This gives an egg-shell gloss. For a dull finish, rub the varnish after it has become bone dry with pulverized pumice stone and water, using a piece of rubbing felt. Rub until the surface is smooth and even, and clean with a wet sponge or chamois skin. If a polished finish is desired, rub first with pulverized pumice stone and water, then with rotten stone and water. Finish with a mixture of oil and a little pulverized rotten stone.

CUTTING TENONS WITH A HAND SAW

This home-made tool will be a great help in the construction of mission furniture. With its use, tenons may be entirely cut with a saw, discarding the use of a chisel and mallet. The device consists of a convenient length of straight board, A, Fig. 1, wide enough to cover the widest piece to be tenoned. A piece of board, B, is fastened to A with brads or small screws. This board should have a thickness equal to the piece to be cut from the side of the tenon. The piece C is fastened to A and B with small cleats at their upper ends. The space between B and C should be wide enough for the blade of a saw to run through easily, and also long enough to take in the widest part of the saw blade. The tool and piece to be tenoned are placed in a vise as shown in Fig. 2. The width of the piece removed for the tenon may be varied by putting in pieces of cardboard between the work, E, and the piece A, Fig. 1.

ARTS AND CRAFTS OIL LAMP

Electricity and gas are not always accessible in suburban or country homes and the regular type of a mission lamp would be of little use. The illustration shows an ordinary round wick kerosene lamp fitted out in mission style.

A few modifications were made in the design of an expensive lamp to simplify the construction. The lamp should have a tall chimney. The dimensions given in the drawings, and the photograph, will explain themselves. Many of the details can be worked up by the maker.

The body of the lamp is made of 1/2-in. oak and is provided with openings as shown. The interior receptacle is very handy for holding a match box, smoking articles, etc.

A piece of copper band, 1 in. wide, is fastened to the body with large upholsterers' tacks, to give it a finished appearance. The base is 7/8 in. thick and in order to prevent tilting is provided with four square feet, 1/4 in. thick. The top piece of the body is 1/2-in. oak, which is provided with a hole large enough to receive the bowl of the lamp. If such a lamp is not at hand, one can be purchased at a very reasonable price.

The shade is made of oak frames set in with clouded art glass panels. The different sections of the frames are fastened together with brass screws and the glass is held in place by triangular cleats of oak. Be sure and fit the shade with cardboard panels before ordering the glass. The cardboard can be used as a pattern in cutting the glass, and the glass will then fit without recutting, which is quite difficult.

The glass beaded fringe should be of suitable color to harmonize with the finished lamp.

The shade is supported by four brackets cast in bronze from a wood pattern (dimensions given) and finished by filing, buffing and lacquering.

ANOTHER CHINA CLOSET

The china closet shown in the accompanying illustration is well proportioned and of pleasing appearance. It can be made of any one of the several furniture woods in common use, but quarter-sawed oak will be found to give the most pleasing effect. The stock should be ordered from the mill ready sawed to length, squared and sanded. In this way much hard labor will be saved. The following pieces will be needed:

1 top, 1 by 19 by 38 in., S-1-S.
4 posts, 3/4 by 3 by 59 in., S-2-S.
4 side rails, 3/4 by 3 by 31 in., S-1-S.
4 end uprights, 1 by 2 by 48-1/2 in., S-2-S.
4 end rails, 1 by 3 by 16 in., S-2-S.
2 lattice rails, 1 by 2 by 13 in., S-2-S.
1 top board, 3/4 by 3 by 36 in., S-1-S.
4 side door rails, 3/4 by 2 by 47 in., S-2-S.
6 cross rails, 3/4 by 2 by 12 in., S-2-S.
4 slats, 1/2 by 3/4 by 16-1/2 in., S-2-S.

4 slats, 1/2 by 3/4 by 13-1/2 in., S-2-S.
8 slats, 1/2 by 3/4 by 12-1/2 in., S-2-S.
4 shelves, 5/8 by 16 by 32 in., S-1-S., poplar.
4 cleats, 1 in. sq. by 55 in., soft wood.
4 cleats, 1 in. sq. by 28 in., soft wood.
4 cleats, 1 in. sq. by 14 in., soft wood.

Having this material on hand, start with the four posts, as they are all alike. Clamp them together, being careful to have them of the right length, and the ends square. Trim the bottom, as shown in the detail drawing, and then lay out the mortises for the front and back rails. These rails can now be laid out and the tenons cut to fit the mortises in the posts. The back rails should, in addition, be rabbeted for the back board as shown. The end rails are fastened to the posts by means of screws through 1-in. square cleats, fastened on the inside of the posts as shown in the section A-A. In all cases the screws should be run through the cleats into the framing so the heads will not show. The end rails should be rabbeted on the inside for the latticework and the glass.

The back board should have the corners rounded as shown and be fastened to the top board with screws through from the bottom side. The top board is then fastened to the top rail cleats in the same manner.

The doors are put together by means of tenons and mortises. The frames should be rabbeted on the inside for the latticework and the glass. Leaded glass can be used in place of this latticework, if it is desired. Suitable hinges and a catch should be supplied. These can be purchased at any hardware store.

The shelves should be cut out at the corners to fit around the cleats. They rest on small blocks which are fastened to the cleats, or if desired, small holes can be drilled and pins used instead.

The back is put on in the usual manner. A mirror can be put in without much trouble if it is desired.

When putting the frame together, glue should be used on the joints, as it makes them much stiffer. Be careful to get the frame together perfectly square, or it will be hard to fit the doors and the glass. When it is complete, go over the whole carefully with fine sandpaper and remove all rough spots. Scrape all the surplus glue from about the joints, as stain will not take when there is any glue. The closet can be finished in any one of the many mission stains supplied by the trade for this purpose.

PART VI. AN OAK BEDSTEAD

AN OAK BEDSTEAD

The accompanying sketches show an artistic design for a mission bed, so simple in construction and design that most any one that has a few tools and a knowledge of their use can make it. It is best made of quarter-sawed oak, as this wood is the easiest to procure and work up and looks well with any finish. If the stock is ordered from the mill ready cut to length, squared and sanded, much of the hard labor will be saved.

The following is a list of the material needed:

2 posts, 2-1/2 by 2-1/2 by 50 in.
2 posts, 2-1/2 by 2-1/2 by 44 in.
2 end rails, 1 by 6 by 56 in.
2 side rails, 1 by 6 by 78 in.
5 end rails, 1 by 4 by 56 in.
3 end rails, 1 by 2 by 56 in.
8 vertical slats, 3/8 by 6 by 11-1/2 in.
10 vertical slats, 3/8 by 2 by 11-1/2 in.
2 cleats, 1 by 1 by 78 in.
5 slats, 3/4 by 3 by 55-1/2 in.
20 blocks, 1 by 1 by 3 in.

Square up the four posts in pairs and lay out the mortises as per drawing. To do this, lay them side by side on a flat surface with the ends square and mark them with a try-square. The tenons on the end rails are laid out in the same manner as the posts. Four of the end rails should be marked and mortises cut for the upright slats as shown in the detail drawing. The tenons on the end rails are about 1 in. long, while those on the slats can be 3/4 in. long. Fit all the parts together before gluing to see that they fit square and tight. After the glue has been applied clamp them together perfectly square and set them away to dry. They should dry at least twenty-four hours before the clamps are removed.

While the ends are drying, the side rails can be made. These have a 1-in. square cleat screwed to the inner side for the slats to rest upon. If springs are used, five slats will be sufficient. They can be placed where the springs will rest upon them. After the position of the slats has been located, nail small blocks at their sides to hold them in place. For fastening the side rails to the posts, patent devices can be purchased at a local hardware store. The posts will have to be mortised to receive these, and care should be exercised to get them in the right place.

When the bed is complete go over it carefully and scrape all the surplus glue from about the joints, as the finish will not take where there is any glue. Remove all rough spots with fine sandpaper; then apply the stain you like best, which may be any of the many mission stains supplied by the trade for this purpose. If this bed is well made and finished, it will be an ornament to any home.

AN OAK FOOTSTOOL

The footstool shown in the illustration can be made from any kind of wood, but when it is intended to be finished in mission style, quarter-sawed oak will produce the best effect. The material needed will be as follows:

1 top, 1 by 9-1/2 by 12 in., S-1-S.

2 legs, 3/4 by 8 by 12 in., S-2-S.

1 brace, 3/4 by 7 by 9 in., S-1-S.

Order these pieces cut to length, squared and sanded. A full-sized layout of the front view should be made to get the correct bevels for the legs and brace. The design of the legs can be varied to suit the fancy of the maker. For such a design as shown draw one-half of it on paper; fold on the center line and with scissors cut both sides of the outline by following the lines drawn. Trace around this pattern on the wood, and saw out with a compass or keyhole saw. The sawed edges should be smoothed and sandpapered.

The perforation in the top board is made by first boring holes, then trimming out the edges with a sharp chisel. Be sure to get the best side of the board up.

The legs are fastened to the top and to the braces with 1-3/4-in. wood screws as shown in the detail drawing. After the stool is assembled, go over it carefully with fine sandpaper and remove all rough spots before applying the finish. This finish can be any one of the many different kinds supplied by the trade for this purpose. If this stool is well made and finished, it will be a useful and attractive article.

A LIBRARY SET IN PYRO CARVING

The multitude of indifferently executed small articles which followed the introduction of pyrography is beginning to disappear, people are considering the art more seriously and applying it to more dignified uses. Pyro-carving is one of the new methods of decorating furniture which is both beautiful and practical, two qualities which do not always go together.

The library set illustrated consists of a table, 30 by 50 in., with two benches, 14 in. wide of the same length. The supports are made of selected white pine, which must be absolutely free from pitch. The pine is soft enough to work easily with the point and stands wear much better than basswood. The tops and braces are made of curly fir, all of the material must be 2-in. lumber, which dresses to about an inch and a half. All surfaces, except the faces of the supports, are given a well-rubbed coat of oil with a little burnt umber, the stain to be applied directly to the wood without a filler.

On the outside of the supports the design is drawn in with pencil, the background is then cut out smoothly with a chisel to the depth of an eighth of an inch, leaving the decoration in relief. It is then burned deeply, the background in straight flat strokes, the outlines having the effect of a sloping, dark edge. The shadows are burned in as deeply as possible and the shading is put in with the flat of the point.

A wax or egg-shell oil varnish finish is most suitable for this set.

A GRILLE WITH PEDESTALS TO MATCH

The accompanying sketch shows something unique in a grille that adds to the appearance of a home furnished in mission style. When it is stained and finished to match the furniture, it gives a consummate tone that would be difficult to obtain by any other means.

To get the best results it should be made to blend with the furniture and the arch in which it is to fit, in both weight and style. This will depend very much upon one's preference, and for this reason full dimensions are not given. No difficulty will be experienced, however, by anyone handy with tools, in making it.

The material should be quarter-sawed oak, which can be secured planed and sanded at the mill. For the grille order 1 by 1-1/2-in. and 1/2 by 1-1/2-in. stock. The method of making the bars is shown in the detailed sketch. The two end bars should be made of solid pieces, 3/4 by 1-1/2 in., with two rectangular slots mortised in each to receive the supports. The supports should be just the right length to go in the arch. To erect, slip the end bars on the supports, hold the grille in place and fasten the bars to the sides of the arch with screws.

The size of the pedestals and the connecting pieces will depend upon the size of the arch. These connecting pieces should be well mortised into the post, and if you own your own home and intend the pedestals to become a fixture, they should also be mortised into the sides of the arch. If not, they may be fastened to the arch with blind screws. The amount of material required will depend upon the size of the arch.

A LADY'S WRITING DESK

This desk of mission style is a little more complicated than some of the other pieces of mission furniture that have been described, but anyone who has a fair knowledge of tools will not have much trouble in constructing it in the home workshop if the plans are carefully followed. Quarter-sawed oak is the best wood to use, as it is easy to work and looks best when finished. Order the stock from the mill ready cut to length, squared and sanded. Following is a list of the stock needed:

2 front posts, 2 by 2 by 30 in.
2 back posts, 2 by 2 by 50 in.
1 bottom rail, 3/4 by 3 by 31 in.
2 end rails, 3/4 by 3 by 18 in.
1 stretcher, 3/4 by 8 by 33-1/2 in.
2 end slats, 3/8 by 8 by 15 in.
1 back slat, 3/8 by 8 by 15-1/2 in.
2 back slats, 3/8 by 3 by 15-1/2 in.
1 front drawer rail, 3/4 by 1-1/4 by 31-1/4 in.
2 side drawer rails, 3/4 by 3 by 18-1/4 in.
1 drawer front, 3/4 by 6 by 30 in.
1 desk lid, 3/4 by 18 by 31-1/4 in.
1 desk board, 3/4 by 19-1/4 by 31-1/4 in.
2 end boards, 3/4 by 19 by 21-1/4 in.
1 top board, 3/4 by 10 by 34 in.
1 top back board, 3/4 by 5 by 31-1/4 in.
1 back board, 3/4 by 30 by 22 in.
2 drawer sides, 1/2 by 6 by 19-1/2 in., S.W.
1 drawer end, 1/2 by 6 by 29 in., S.W.
1 drawer bottom, 1/2 by 18 by 29 in., S.W.
2 pieces for pigeon holes, 3/8 by 7 by 23 in., S.W.
8 pieces for pigeon holes, 3/8 by 4 by 6-3/4 in., S.W.

Start with the back posts, being sure they are square and of the right length; place them side by side and lay out the mortises for the lower rails, the desk rails and the top back boards, as shown in the accompanying detail drawing. Lay out the front posts in the same manner. Cut the tenons on the ends of the rails to fit the mortises in the posts. Also cut mortises in the rails for the back and end slats. The end rails have a mortise in them for the tenons on the ends of the foot boards. Clamp the ends of the desk together, with the end rails in place; then fit the side boards. Bore holes through the posts into the side boards for dowels as shown. After the dowels are in place the holes can be plugged.

Cut and fit the top back board, the bottom rail, the back board and the stretcher. Cut the top and desk boards at the back corners to clear the posts. The top board is to be fastened to the side boards with blind screws. The back board is fastened to the posts with dowels as shown.

When all the parts fit square and tight they can be glued together. The ends of the desk should be glued up first and left to dry, then the other parts put in place and glued. When clamping the parts together see that they fit perfectly square and tight. While the glue is drying the drawer can be made. The front board is made of oak, but the other parts may be made of some soft wood. The side pieces are mortised and glued to the front board, The end and bottom boards can be nailed together.

The drop lid of the desk is made as shown. Two or more boards may have to be glued together for the lid, the desk bottom and the back board. The lid is fastened to the desk board with two hinges, and it should be so arranged that when closed it will be even with the sides. Brackets or chains are fastened to the inside to hold it in the proper position when it is open. Small blocks of wood fastened to the inner edge of the side boards will prevent it from closing too far. A lock, if desired, can be purchased at a hardware store and fitted in place. Suitable handles for the drawer should also be provided.

When the desk is complete go over it with fine sandpaper and remove all rough spots. Scrape all glue from about the joints, as the finish will not take where there is any glue.

The pigeonholes are made from 3/8-in. stock. They may be tacked in place after the desk is finished.

The finish can be any one of the many mission stains supplied by the trade for this purpose. If the desk is well made and finished, it will have a very neat and attractive appearance.

A TELEPHONE STAND AND STOOL

The stand shown in the accompanying illustration is for use with a desk telephone. The stool when not in use, slides on two runners under the stand. A shelf is provided for the telephone directory, paper, pencil, etc.

The joints may be made with dowels, or the mortise and tenon may be used, as desired. If the latter is decided upon, allowance must be made on the length of the rails for the tenons. The list given is for the dowel-made joints. The following stock list gives the amount of material needed which should be ordered planed and sanded. This work can be done by hand if the builder has the time and desires to have an entire home-made article. However, the list is given for the mill-planed material.

Stand

4 posts, 1-1/2 in. square by 29 in.
2 rails, 7/8 by 5 by 11 in.
1 rail, 7/8 by 1-1/2 by 13 in.
1 rail, 7/8 by 5 by 13 in.
2 runners, 7/8 by 1-1/2 by 14 in.
1 top, 7/8 by 18 by 20 in.
1 shelf, 7/8 by 12-7/8 by 13-3/4 in.

Stool

4 posts, 1-1/2 in. square by 17 in.
4 rails, 7/8 by 4 by 6-1/2 in.
4 rails, 7/8 by 2 by 6-1/2 in.
1 stretcher, 7/8 by 4 by 7-1/4 in.
1 top, 7/8 by 12-1/2 in. square.

The exact lengths for the posts are given in the list. Should the builder desire to square them up, allowance must be made for this when ordering stock.

Arrange all the pieces in the position they are to occupy in the finished stand and stool and number all the joints. Locate the centers and bore holes for all the dowels. Assemble the two sides of the table first. Notch the runners and fasten them to the posts with flat-head screws. Use hot glue on the dowel joints if possible.

Cut the corners out of the shelf to fit the legs and assemble the frame of the table. Use round-head screws through the rails to hold the shelf. The top may be fastened in two ways, with screws through cleats on the inside of the rails and under the top, or with screws slanting through the upper part of the rails and into the top as shown. The stool, is assembled in the same manner as the stand.

The stand and stool should be finished to harmonize with the furniture and woodwork of the room in which they are to be used.

PART VII. HOW TO MAKE A DOWEL CUTTING TOOL

HOW TO MAKE A DOWEL CUTTING TOOL

Secure a piece of steel about 1/4 in. thick, 1-3/4 in. wide and 8 in. long. Drill various sized holes through the steel as shown in Fig. 1, leaving the edge of each hole as sharp as the drill will make them. Cut off a block of wood the length necessary for the dowels and split it up into pieces about the size for the particular dowel to be used. Lay the steel on something flat, over a hole of some kind, then start one of the pieces of wood in the proper size hole for the dowel and drive it through with a hammer, as shown in Fig. 2. The sharp edges on the steel will cut the dowel as smooth and round as if it were turned in a lathe.

A MEDICINE CABINET

This cabinet is best made of quarter-sawed oak, as this wood is the most easily procured and looks well when finished. Order the stock from the mill ready cut to length, squared and sanded. The following pieces will be needed:

4 posts, 1-1/2 by 1-1/2 by 28 in.
4 side rails, 3/4 by 2 by 16 in.
4 end rails, 3/4 by 2 by 7 in.
2 door rails, 3/4 by 2 by 15 in.
2 door rails, 3/4 by 2 by 22-3/4 in.
1 door panel, 1/4 by 11-1/2 by 19-1/4 in.
1 back panel, 1/4 by 15-1/2 by 23-1/4 in.
2 end panels, 1/4 by 6-1/2 by 23-1/4 in.

2 pieces for top and bottom, 1/2 by 6-3/4 by 15-3/4 in.

Square the four posts and bevel the tops as shown.

Cut grooves in them with a plow plane to receive the 1/4-in. panels. The tenons on the rails are cut 1/4 in. wide and fit into the grooves in the posts the same as the panels. The rails have grooves cut at the inside edges for the panels. The front posts do not have grooves on the inside but have two mortises, one at each end for the top and bottom rails. The back has a panel fitted in the same as the ends. See that the pieces fit together perfectly square and tight, then glue them together and give it time to dry.

The top and bottom boards are next put in place. The top is placed in the center of the top rails while the bottom is put even with the lower edge of the bottom rails, as shown in the detail drawing. The door frame is mitered at the corners and rabbeted on the inner edge to take the panel. A mirror can be used in place of the panel if desired. Suitable hinges and a catch, which can be purchased at a hardware store, should be supplied for the door.

The shelves are of soft wood and are to be arranged to suit the maker. Before applying a finish, go over the cabinet with fine sandpaper and remove all the surplus glue about the joints and the rough spots, else the finish will not take evenly. The finish can be any one of the many different kinds supplied by the trade for this purpose.